Why Craigslist is Better than eBay!
How to Post and Sell Items on Craigslist Safely and Successfully

By
James E. Britton

Copyright © 2016 by James E. Britton
All rights reserved. This book or any portion thereof may not be reproduced or used in any manner whatsoever without the express written permission of the publisher except for the use of brief quotations in a book review.
Printed in the United States of America
ISBN: 9781520100722

Table Of Contents:

Chapter One: Why Craigslist?

Chapter Two: What Can You Sell on Craigslist?

Chapter Three: Strategies For Selling

Chapter Four: Selling FAQs

Chapter Five: How to Safely Negotiate the Seller Contact Sequence

Chapter Six: The Finish Line

Chapter One: Why Craigslist?

Craigslist is a site for buyers and sellers, which perhaps you've heard more about than actually tried. Or maybe you interacted with it a little bit: with mixed or less than desirable results. But......what about that nagging feeling you may have that you may be missing out on opportunities because you didn't know enough about it to explore its fullest potential?

Craigslist is a site that can be utilized for a multitude of things. Everything from finding a job, to trying to fill a job opening, to chatting about common issues, finding a new bandmate, a new apartment, a new roommate, a new house or simply a place to find a great deal on something you are looking to buy, or a way to make a few extra dollars selling things you don't need any more.

Well, that's not all Craigslist is. It's a marketplace, an open bartering system for people trying to make deals. It's not just buying and selling yard sale junk. There are people who use Craigslist to make a living. Real estate agents use it to enhance their listing processes. Investors and scammers alike are trolling the internet everywhere looking for partners (or in the case of the latter maybe victims...) If the internet is a web then surely Craig's list is its net with millions of trawlers every day casting their lines hoping to catch their fish. I wouldn't worry about the scammers too much; a few common sense measures will immunize you from their schemes. We'll talk more about that later on.

Opportunities are abundant on Craigslist. But so, too, are risks. So let's talk about this a little bit. This eBook mostly represents the point of view of the seller, and I will share advice the best advice I can give on how to sell as efficiently as possible on Craigslist.

Let me first begin with an explanation about how I came to write this book. Back in 2001, my wife and I were on the frontier of selling on eBay. Why am I talking about eBay in a book dedicated to Craigslist (also known as CL)? That deserves its own explanation. There are many similarities and differences between CL and eBay, so let me share with you the story of how we moved (mostly) away from eBay to sell on CL.

Back then, eBay was like the wild, wild, west. In those days, eBay was an auction only site, so people always had to bid to "win" a particular item. eBay eventually evolved to add features like "Buy it Now", eBay Stores and "Fixed Price" listings. These methods of selling developed in response to the overwhelming frustration expressed by eBay users who were disappointed because they were getting "sniped" at the last minute by buyers who would bid at the last second to win an auction. In fact, there were even "sniping" services which grew on the internet that would automatically place bids for you at the last second.

People were tired of having to sit at their computer waiting for the exact second an auction ended, and constantly having to refresh their browser pages. They were hoping not to get outbid, or to get in a higher bid at the last second if they noted that there was someone else out there watching the same auction at its close. Users continued to expressed their frustration to eBay and reinforced in their feedback to the company that they wanted to buy things when and at the price they wanted.

On the other side of the equation, we as sellers were making a killing in the early days of eBay. People were paying ridiculous prices for items that we had just hanging around the house or that could be found commonly at garage sales. It wasn't too long before others were discovering that they too could make extra cash, and in some cases, make a living selling things on eBay.

Fast forward ten years later, and everybody had begun copycatting everybody else. Niches no longer begat riches. Amazon started selling items that we had begun purchasing wholesale. Our customers did the same, and soon became competitors. Our customers were buying things from us, finding out who the wholesaler was, and then opening their own account to sell. eBay eventually increased their seller's fees. Feedback wars were not uncommon, if either buyer or seller were not completely satisfied. Once Amazon started offering free shipping, sellers on eBay soon followed. eBay was becoming a much more competitive marketplace for sellers.

In response to these customer requests, eBay began to experiment with fixed price "auctions." After some tweaking they were considered to be a great success, and ultimately were the foundation of how eBay stores came to be. It is now more the exception than the rule that items on eBay are sold through the traditional auction process.

Shipping and customer problems, as well as diminishing profits and seller constant seller unfriendly policy changes by eBay made us finally make a decision to get the heck out. EBay had become more trouble than it was worth. Fees were too high. Customer demands were ridiculous, by and large the scene had become all about penny pinchers kicking tires to get something for nothing, and sellers as competitors who ignored their own labor costs willing to sell things for next to no profit and ship for free.

If you weigh the ship for free phenomenon in comparison to the continued increase in costs from shipping providers, it makes for even more of a losing equation. That is why we decided that eBay was largely no longer for us. Do we still sell things on eBay? Yes-but we try to stay out of the shipping game as much as possible. eBay is the second choice. When something doesn't sell on Craigslist, then, and only then do we move items on to eBay with certain exceptions which I will explain shortly.

We sell as much as possible through Craig's list, and, because our items require local pickup we largely do not engage in the shipping game nightmare. We live in an extremely rural part of New Hampshire-but if we do a good job of finding and advertising items people truly want, people are willing to make the effort to come and get them. Sometimes we will negotiate to make a delivery, but only if we are certain the transaction will be completed.

Of course this doesn't work for everything, and for those things that won't sell on Craigslist it is garage sale or EBay time. We prefer to save our items and then offer them at one large garage sale, rather than selling them one at a time. Over the course of time we have become much savvier at what we buy, so as to minimize the need for the garage sale close-outs. Our last choice is to sell on eBay. The most recent thing I sold on eBay cost almost $ 10 to ship, and a fair amount of time to package, not to mention eBay's final value fee assessed as a result of successfully transacting on their site.

Net profit : $ 6 for about ½ hour invested on an item that originally was worth well more than the final price. I call it a net profit only because the item in question had zero remaining value to me.

There is one caveat. eBay allows you to list 50 items for free every month. That is one thing that they have done to continue to attract sellers (like me) who might otherwise disappear. If you happen to be in business with someone else-say for example a joint venture to sell goods, then each of you has 50 free listings, assuming you have separate eBay accounts. So my take on it is this: Why not take advantage of this, and list our most expensive items? <u>BUT only allow for local pick-up</u>. Sure that diminishes our odds of selling things, but it can open conversations that lead to compromise or negotiation that might make it worthwhile for delivery. It helps get us out of the free shipping game, and puts some skin in the game for the people who want the item, instead of the onus and expectation that we as the seller have to either ship for free or do cartwheels to make a delivery occur.

When we got to the bottom we will list items and agree to ship them on eBay but that again is : <u>the last resort choice.</u> There are some items we will sell on Amazon as well but generally we consider selling on eBay to selling on Amazon as being roughly equal. Amazon is better for selling books, DVDs, video games, etc. most everything else I would tend to lean towards eBay. And that's not a hard and fast rule. It's a case by case basis as to which portal we think a given item is more likely to sell on. To summarize-here is our business model for selling items on-line:

EBay also has those lovely "Final Value" Fees that are assessed to you once you sell an item. You are giving EBay a 10% cut + if you use PayPal (which most sellers do) it's another 3 % or so. That along with shipping issues are certainly enough reasons to consider other alternatives first!

My take is that the strategy would be to list on eBay ONLY after you have exhausted all the listing that you want to do on Craigslist. People on CL expect items to be for local pickup only, while those on eBay do not. Therefore, your target audience is much more aligned with your audience expectations if you are pursuing a no delivery (or as little as possible) strategy as we follow in our selling practices. One other option is to sell on Amazon, but I have even less luck in that marketplace, unless by chance I happened to have a book that still had some market value. (Usually still very new-prices on books crash quickly and the market in selling books is deathly competitive.)

My goal is to share with you philosophy and best practices, not to provide a bunch of filler information. I am not going to get into a discussion of Craigslist history or how to sign up for an account. I am assuming you can figure basic things like that on your own. As we move from philosophy to practical application, let's look at some specific strategies that will help improve your odds of success as you place your listings on Craigslist.

A small amount of strategy can make a large difference in terms of how likely you are to sell your item, and equally as important, how quickly it sells. The last thing you want to do is to put the effort into creating a listing, taking the pictures etc., etc., and then hoping and praying that it sells. It requires some investment beyond that initial effort in most cases to get an item sold. That is the difference between the average CraigLister and the ones who succeed.

If you create a listing and then do nothing else you might sell something once in a while, but like any other activity you can't just make a token effort and expect the phone to ring. So, let's explore some proactive strategies that will increase the likelihood that your listing will get seen, which will increase your chances of getting an item sold.

Chapter Two: What Can You Sell on Craigslist?

Before we get into strategies for selling, let's first take a look at some ideas for what kind of products or services that we might want to sell on Craigslist, and where we might find them.

1 Free!-Search the Free Category in Craigslist-you'll be surprised what you find there, and some items with a little TLC can be fixed up and re-sold for a decent profit.

2. Thrift Stores-Many thrift stores don't have time to research the value of the items they sell, they are interested in moving items quickly. Many bargains can be had if you have an eye for or knowledge about certain items which you know you can re-sell for a decent return.

3. Cleaning Homes & Businesses-an obvious service based business that can build clientele from listing on Craigslist.

4. Create and sell your OWN crafts or products. If you have a creative flair, or a knack for making things this might be worth considering. One of the greatest things about creating your OWN items is that you don't have to pay anyone else for inventory. If your item is unique enough you may find there is not much competition. The trick is that you have to make something that people are willing to pay for, and that gives you a decent return on your investment of time in the creation process. (Don't make the mistake of undervaluing your time. If you spend three hours making something that people will pay you $ 15 for-you didn't just make $ 15 profit. You made $ 5 per hour minus your time to market and meet with the buyer etc. That's not a very good return on investment.)

5. Lawn mowing, shoveling snow, landscaping or any other similar service.

6. Moving (Rent a truck and start moving things for people).

7. Marketing for business owners who are not internet savvy or who do not have time to do it for themselves.

8. Buy wholesale and re-sell. There are whole books written about this. Google Retail Arbitrage and you will find volumes of information on how this works.

9. Outsource graphic design or web site work.

10. "Must Sell" Items. There are people who are trying to sell thing on Craigslist in your local area that are desperate for cash and need to sell something TODAY and state as such in their ads. If they really are desperate, they're ready to make a deal. Try inputting the search phrase "must sell today" or "need to sell today" on Craigslist, you may be surprised by what you find!

Chapter Three: Strategies For Selling

So let's get into the strategies for selling:

1. Keep Your Ad on Top!

This first strategy is the gospel of CL: Keep Your Ad on Top! You must keep re-posting if you want people to see your CL ad. Craigslist is similar to Google. The further down the results page your ad appears the less likely people are to see it. People HATE scrolling pages, so if you aren't on the first and to some degree, the second page, you might as well be invisible. If you haven't had a response in a few days, then you should definitely think about re-listing your ad.

Free classified posts on Craigslist can be **renewed**. Renewing a post will move that post to the top of the list.

You can renew an active free post as long as 48 hours have elapsed since it was initially posted, or if 48 hours have elapsed since it was last renewed. If you go to your account page on Craigslist, an option (link) to "renew" will appear next to your listing. Using this link as often as CL will allow is the fastest way to make sure your listings remain current. I recommend you check your listings often and watch for the "renew" link to appear next to any of your postings. Every day I go through the list and re-post anything that has that link next to it, at the time of day I want it to be re-posted. It only takes a second to renew a listing and it is worth the effort to keep your listing as close as possible to the top of the page.

Please note that renewing a post will not extend its lifespan, and once a post is 30 days old you will lose the ability to renew it. **For more details on posting lifespans see the chart below. Note that there are different** lifespans for different categories. According to Craigslist "Renewing free posts:

Be aware that postings expire after a certain amount of time. SO if your item has not sold, or you are offering other services, etc. Be aware that your listing will only last for so long"

Expirations by Posting Type

Posting Type	Expires
Jobs	30 days
Free: For Sale, Housing, Personals, Services, Community	7-45 days*
Gigs, Resumes	30-45 days*
Events	Depends
Paid: NYC broker apartments	30 days
Paid: Cars & Trucks by Dealer, Tickets by Dealer	30 days
Paid: Therapeutic	7 days

* varies by city

(Source: Craigslist website)

The fast and easy way to re-post is to simply click on the edit this posting button. Make any changes (if any) if you have none you still have to hit the edit this posting button if you wish to re-new it. I prefer to wait the 48 hours because it I much simpler than copying and pasting and you don't have to re-load your images.

The below picture shows what the screen looks like when you go to re-new an ad. Click on the "Edit this Posting" button-even if you don't intend to make any edits. Then just follow the process as if this were a new listing-the difference being that all the info and pictures are already there for you! You can of course make edits at this time if you choose to do so.

> Your posting can be seen at http://nh.craigslist.org/msg/5665590632.html.
>
> [Edit this Posting]   You can make changes to the content of your post.
> [Update Images]   Add or remove images attached to this posting
> [Edit Location]   Change how this posting appears on a map.
> [Delete this Posting] This will remove your posting from active listing.

(Source: Craigslist web site)

However, be aware that renewing a post will not extend its lifespan, and **once a post is 30 days old you will lose the ability to renew it.** It is extremely important to be aware of this. When you notice that the "re-new" option no longer appears next to your postings, you should re-post it as a new listing. If "re-new" option no longer appears next to your postings, then follow the Manual Re-List Instructions below.

Manual Re-List Instructions:

If you don't want to wait the 48 hours, or your post is 30 days old you can manually re-list your ad fairly quickly. Be aware that If you try to post something similar to an active post of yours on the site, you may get a blocked message. Removing the similar active post should help, unless it is less than 48 hours old. Here's how to manually re-list if you wish to do this:

A.) Prepare to post your initial ad as you would usually do.

B.) When you are ready, log into your account again, do a right click on the listing you want to re-new and open it in a new window or tab.

C.) Now, at the top left of the new tab you just opened you will see the category it is in (it is in the top left, in the shaded area.) Highlight the Category that you have listed your posting, and open it in a new tab, or new window. REMEMBER to HIGHLIGHT the Category first, and then right click to choose the option to open in a new window.

D.) Now, select the **POST** button on the RH side. Then choose a category, and then a location. (Again, this is the shaded area at the top RH side of the page.)

E. Next, go back to the tab or window that you opened that has your existing ad in it. Copy and paste the contents of your ad into the new listing template. Yes, you will have to re-load any pictures you have-so keep your pictures organized in a file where you know you can find them quickly, and easily!

F. Follow the usual steps for completing your posting.

G. It will take an indefinite amount of time for your new ad to appear. Sometimes Craigslist is updated right away sometime not. Keep checking back until you see your new listing. According to CL it should be about 15 minutes. Sometimes they will also send you an e-mail which you will have to click on where indicated before your ad will be published. Then, MAKE SURE to go back and delete your original listing. Your ad should now be back at the top of the category. (I have found that if I don't go back and delete the original listing it confuses me sometimes. There's no sense competing with yourself by trying to sell the same item twice!)

2. Make sure that you post the best possible pictures!

Many people search Craigslist either using the catalog view, or the thumbnail view. Probably the single most important thing other than the headline is your leading image. Craigslist now allows you to post up to 24 pictures, include as many pictures as necessary as to accurately portray your item.

Makes sure you pick the best possible image to be the one that is featured. The more pictures you display the better, especially if it is a larger item. It is not necessary to invest in an expensive camera. In this day and age most smartphones take high quality pictures. There is no reason to not include good photographs. In fact, some shoppers may assume you have something to hide if you don't include good quality pictures.

As far as taking the pictures themselves, taking pictures in natural light (daylight) usually works well. It also helps to take pictures against a solid color background. I often lay my items on a bedspread because it provides a solid consistent background. Some items are better taken vertically, so standing them up in front of a hanging sheet or solid colored wall also looks good. Check your pictures as you take them, and tweak whatever necessary until you get the shots that come out the way you want them. Don't compromise here-a good quality picture will do wonders for your listing!

3. Make your listing as detailed as possible:

Ultimately, your item has to be desirable enough for someone to not just pay for it, but ideally, to also want to come and get it. (If it's a common item, you better have a pretty good price to motivate someone to want to come and get it!) People want to know as much as they can about something before they make the commitment to buy something, so add as much as you can about your item-especially if it involves the condition of the item.

Also, use HTML code in your ads to make them stand out more. Craigslist allows you to use some simple HTML codes, and they can make a difference to making your ad look unique. If you are not familiar with HTML codes, this is a not a necessity. It's simply a way of adding things like bold, italics, underlining or color to an ad.

For more information on what HTML codes Craigslist allows, click on the following link:

https://www.craigslist.org/about/help/html_in_craigslist_postings/details

4. Make sure you do your research HOMEWORK before posting.

This is one thing that eBay is very good for. If you have an item to sell, scan eBay for similar items–chances are you'll find something that is at least similar in some way.

There are a lot of things up on eBay that sometimes people ask crazy prices for; just to see if someone is foolish enough to pay it. But a look at the open listings is worth the effort as it will give you some ballpark figures to create a price range. Just don't be foolish enough to think that just because someone lists something at a high price that the item is worth that to potential buyers. For the most accurate market evaluations take a look at the **SOLD** listings. The SOLD listings are the price someone was actually willing to pay.

These days, the free shipping phenomenon has taken everyone by storm-so don't forget to account for what shipping might be. For example, an item that is listed for $30 that costs the seller $15 to ship that is listed as having "Free Shipping" has an actual value of $ 15. Don't assume because it's listed on eBay it's worth the $30 they have it listed for.

As you are doing your search, there is one website I want to bring to your attention that can help make your search more thorough. SearchTempest (http://www.searchtempest.com/) will search all of Craigslist, eBay & more in one search. (I am not an affiliate of theirs nor do I gain anything by mentioning them, I just think they're a great tool, much as I feel about Google AdWords).

SearchTempest is a search engine for online classified ads. They bring together results from all of Craigslist, eBay, and Amazon, as well as many other sites. It's easy to find what you want when you can search multiple cities and all the top classifieds sites at once. (It's great for finding things if you are looking to buy something as well.)

SearchTempest uses a Google Custom Search to search for Craigslist ads matching your search, and then provides links to those ads, which open in new windows, directly from Craigslist. By default they organize the results by city, starting with the ones nearest to you, but you can change to one of several other sort options. They also use APIs from eBay, Amazon, and Oodle, to find results for your search.
(Application program interface (API) is a set of routines, protocols, and tools for building software applications. An API specifies how software components should interact and APIs are used when programming graphical user interface (GUI) components.) APIs are nothing you need to know about, I just included that info for those inclined to be interested in such things.

Once you have a general sense of what the market is willing to pay, and also a sense of what other the item is selling for, you will have some idea of what price to ask for yours. Remember eBay is an international market, so I would say it's safe to assume that the prices you see on eBay would be lower than what you might see in your local market. However, when setting your price, don't be afraid to err on the higher side, for two reasons:

A: It is easier to reduce your price than to increase it. Once you list a price, you are somewhat locked into setting an upper limit on its value. (Unless of course you find out it's worth more and you want to re-list it before you sell it too cheaply. Not a frequent occurrence, I am sure, but sometimes it does happen.)

B: You have to provide some room for people to haggle. People are always looking for bargains, and many is the time when someone will ask you if you would take a lower price for your item. The feeling that someone is getting a good deal is much more likely to make someone make the effort to purchase your item. If you list it at your rock bottom price you may not be able to sell it, especially if you insist on selling without any negotiation.

If you really want to move an item you can suggest that you are willing to accept the best offer for the item. If you do this, I suggest also putting in a time frame. For example: For sale $ 25 or Best Offer received by Friday July 29. That way there is a push to action on the part of the person who might be making an offer.

When you make a sale on Craigslist make sure that you — accept CASH only, preferably in $20 bills or less. Any other form of payment is up to you, but it is at your risk. On Craigslist cash is king, and most buyers have learned to accept that.

5. Another Strategy: Bundling

Retailers are notorious for this. How many times have you seen things bundled together? It's the old "this goes with that-so why not get both at the same time?" In a retail environment it is also sometimes known as "cross-merchandising." That is why you see corkscrews hanging in the wine aisle, or a wine display in the cheese section. Your intent may have been to buy some good cheese, but through the power of suggestion...suddenly you realize how great a nice bottle of wine would be to go with it! Fast food restaurants do this all the time by offering "combo meals" with several items bundled together for a single price.

You can take advantage of this strategy-If you have items that go together why not list them together? Hmm....pair of old skates, and this hockey stick I have hanging around...If you think selling items separately will bring you more money, then by all means do so. But as an example, I closed a deal on selling a drum set by being willing to include two sets of drum sticks with it. Be creative, maybe there is something you can do to sell two (or more) items at once!

6. About Communication

Be aware that some buyers will send e-mails out to several sellers if they see an identical or similar item on Craigslist. Sometimes the person who responds the quickest is the one who gets the sale. That is one reason to respond to your e-mail inquiries as soon as you can.

Provide Appropriate Contact Info:

There are plenty of stories about Craigslist scams, but they are not as common as the media might have you believe. Most importantly, be smart about how much information you make available for potential buyers. I don't like to provide my phone number, but some people do, because they insist they get better results when people can text them. Personally, I think e-mail is fine. I do make sure that I use the Craigslist feature to anonymize my e-mail address.

For your peace of mind, perhaps an explanation as to how the Craigslist "anonymous e-mail" feature works is in order:

"Craigslist has implemented 2-way email relay to help stop spam and scams.
When replying to a post you'll see an address like:
abcde-0123456789@sale.Craigslist.org
When answering an email you'll see an address like:
rcc9la26d7534400a6a03514c34f9200@reply.Craigslist.org
Use your email program as you normally would.

PLEASE NOTE: The "real name" field (e.g. Jane Doe) in your email program is passed through to the recipient. Any contact information in the body of your message will pass through unaltered."

(Source: Craigslist website)

I have tested this and it works. If you have assigned a real name to your e-mail account they will see that, but they will never see your real e-mail address (and vice versa) unless you specifically give it to them.

Don't "Hold" Items:

If you happen to have an item that is in high demand, you may get several e-mails in a short period of time. You may get someone who asks if you can "hold" an item until they can get to your location. Unfortunately if they never show up-this is not that unusual-you end up holding on to an item that you might have been otherwise able to sell. It is better to operate on a first come first served basis. Whoever arrives with the cash first is the one who gets the item!

Save Your Emails:

Even when I have an interested buyer that seems like close to a sure thing, I save e-mails from any other potential buyers who have expressed interest. That way if the first buyer end up being a no-show I still have contact info for the others as back-ups.

7. Product Description

It's a good idea to keep your description simple and clean. Bulleted lists outlining features usually come across well, and are easy for the potential buyer to read. It may also be relevant to include details about why you're selling it. I like to do this, as I feel it lends credibility to my listing. Read your description back as if you were the buyer. What questions would you ask before you made the purchase?

It's also good to include keywords in your description. Craigslist's search feature will not only search the title but also the description.

Tell Why You Are Selling the Item.

People want to know why you're selling your item. They want to make sure you're not just trying to dump a lemon on them. Here are some reasons that you are selling an item that people like to hear:

- You are moving.
- You just purchased a new version and don't need this one anymore.
- You gave up golf, or whatever activity is associated with the product, so you don't need the golf clubs anymore.

Giving a good reason makes it clear to prospective buyers that you're not just trying to unload something because it's broken, defective, etc.

There is also a question of whether or not you should list other available items at the end of each item listing. I have heard some con against this, as some people want buyers to think their item is exclusive and unique, and that you are not in the "business" of selling. But, if your items are similar enough, I think it's a good idea. If someone is interested enough in one of your items, they may easily decide to pick up another one or even more, if the items all happen to fit within the general fancy of the interested buyer.

```
┌─ posting details ──────────────────────────────────────────────┐
│                                                                │
│  make / manufacturer        model name / number     size / dimensions │
│  [                  ]       [                  ]    [length x width x height] │
│                                                                │
│  language of posting  condition                                │
│  [english    ▼]      [new    ▼]                                │
│                                                                │
│  include "more ads by this user" link                          │
│  ☐                                                             │
│                                                                │
└────────────────────────────────────────────────────────────────┘
```

If you want potential buyers to be able to see all of your items at once, MAKE SURE to click on the box in the posting details that says "include 'more ads by this user' link. (See illustration above.) That way potential buyers can see your other items, and maybe decide to get more than one item from you. It is sometimes easier to commit to a second (or third etc.) if they know they are already making the effort to connect with you for a purchase.

Feel free to remind your potential buyers that this button exists. It shows up on the RH side of the listing page. I usually put in caps "TO SEE OTHER ITEMS I HAVE FOR SALE, MAKE SURE TO CLICK ON THE "MORE ADS BY THIS USER" LINK."

If you click the "more ads by this user" button on one of your own ads it will take you to a page that lists all of your items. If you copy and paste the URL from your browser window, you can promote that URL on your website, your Facebook page, your Blog, or any other site you wish on the World Wide Web.

condition: **good**

make / manufacturer: **Cannondale**

model name / number: **ST600**

serial number: **sweetvintageride**

size / dimensions: **19" frame/ 28" step over**

more ads by this user

- safety tips
- prohibited items
- product recalls
- avoiding scams

8. Choosing your title

Make sure you use the most relevant terms to describe your item. I sometimes use Google AdWords planner to help me choose keywords. (https://adwords.google.com/KeywordPlanner#start) I don't do that for every item because it is not really time efficient-but for certain items especially if they are higher ticket, or if it is an item I intend to sell multiples of, I like to use a resource to help with choosing relevant title and description keywords. Don't feel like you're missing out if you aren't familiar with AdWords. It is simply a tool like a dictionary or a thesaurus. You can function fine without it, it is simply an additional resource for ideas or inspiration. The point here is to choose a good descriptive title. Ask yourself the question "what keywords would I use if I were looking for an item like this?" If you really want to nail it-take some time to learn about AdWords, especially if you plan to regularly sell items on Craigslist.

The goal when writing an ad title is to get buyers attention, and ultimately, to get them to click on your ad! So how do you do this? Using the old Marketing AIDA formula. AIDA stands for Attention Interest Desire Action. In Marketing, it is a recognized concept that people must move through each of these phases in order to make a successful sale, or from the standpoint of the consumer, make a purchase.

This is not about manipulating people to move through this process. The process is identified, and your job is to help the potential purchaser being easily guided through these steps. Note I say *guided*, not manipulated or coerced. We are not trying to use any sneaky tricks here, we are simply positioning our offering in the best light to make it easier for the consumer to make a decision that will fulfill their needs.

So what makes a good title? First you have to get their attention, then pique their interest. This then must resonate with their own desire. Lastly, you should use a call to action in your title to get them to look at the ad.

Some examples of Call To Action are:

- "Check Us Out"
- "Sale Ends Soon"
- "Love Your Pet!"
- "Check out our great reviews!"
- "See Pictures"
- "Check the offer inside"

Each one of these phrases subtly asks for the viewer to click on the ad to get more information.

Remember that you only get 70 characters to work with. One trick you might use is to put your Call to Action in the Location area of your post instead of wasting that space on a location.

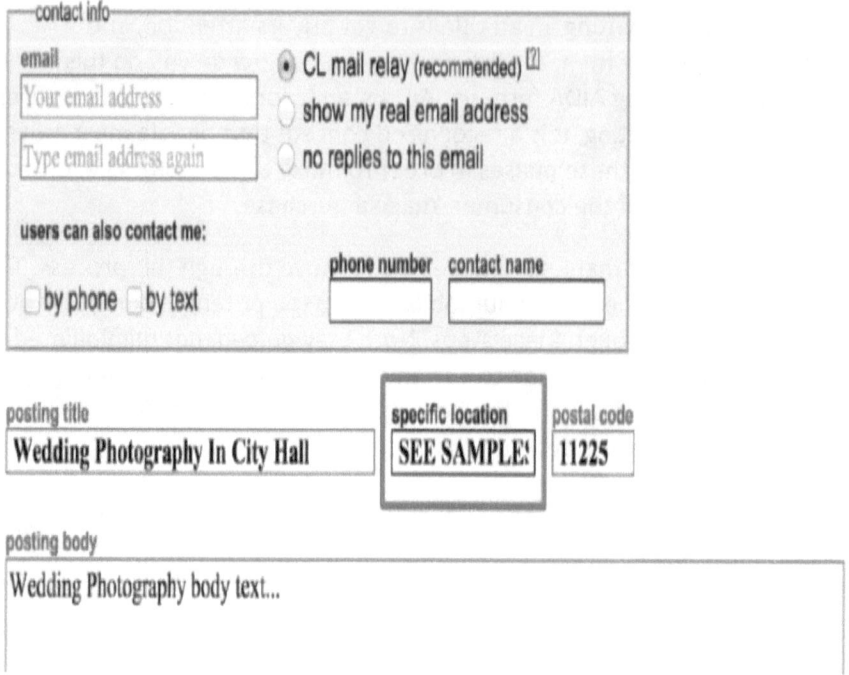

Some cities have sub locations, which will not allow you to do this. However there is way around it:

new york craigslist > manhattan > services > household services > choose neighborhood

choose the location that fits best:

○ Battery Park

○ Chelsea

○ Chinatown / Lit Italy

○ Downtown

○ East Harlem

○ East Village

○ bypass this step
(your posting may not show up in by-location searches)

Must click bypass to have option to enter "specific location"

Other ideas for creating a great title:

Getting their attention:

A. Add a symbol (color if possible): add a symbol to your title, it will make your title stand out. It's actually best to bracket your listing with symbols, as it makes it look more balanced. For example: * Best Price on Craigslist *

B. Use Initial Caps or All Caps. Only use All Caps when title is very short. Initial Caps is when you capitalize every word (except unimportant like, the, if ,and, or but). For example :

> Yellow Ford Pinto Yellow Low Mileage Guaranteed Not to Blow Up if Hit in Rear!

> All Caps are considered to be basically annoying, but if you have a short title it is acceptable to use them. Example:

> **ON SALE NOW 24 HOURS ONLY TIRES FOR $ 5!**

C. Use space as in *---------Here I am-------*: By doing this it sets your item apart from others on Craigslist. By centering your title it makes you stand out in a long list of other titles. This is a very effective technique for getting people to see your ad in a sea of other offerings.
D. Make your title clear and concise and make it different! If your title is the same or similar to others in the same category give some thought to how you can make your ad distinctive and unique.
E. As for the description: Begin with your benefit. What benefit will the purchaser gain as a result of acquiring your item or service?
F. You can list a double benefit! This item will save you money AND make you strong/smart/skinny……whatever.
G. Create curiosity by : Violating Expectations, highlight the information gap that's relevant, and show that the information gap truly exists. What do we mean by "violating expectations?"

What do we mean by "Violating Expectations?" Let's take a quick look at what is known as the "Expectancy Violations Theory. "

"We predict the future based on our schemas and other beliefs we have formed. Having made the prediction, we then expect our predictions to come true. When they do not, an expectancy violation has occurred.

What happens next is that we are surprised. This draws us in, capturing our attention as we try to understand what has happened and perhaps modify our schema to cope with this new situation."

(source: changingminds.com)

You probably already know that most curiosity is triggered by challenging common beliefs.

Imagine you have a headline which reads:

Make More Sales For Your Business By Selling More Items!

This is a really obvious headline, and is does not really do anything to garner the readers interest. What if you instead change the headline to read:

How to Double Your Sales in 20 minutes.

This Violates expectations by suggesting that making a small change can create dramatic results.

You'll often see sites like Copyblogger violating expectations in their headlines. For example:

"There is No ROI in Social Media Marketing"

In this headline there is something readers may not expect. As a result, disorder is created, which requires investigation to restore sense and meaning. The idea being to create enough curiosity in the head of your reader to make them want to take action by investigating further (i.e. click on your ad.)

However, curiosity alone is not enough. To inspire action, you have to violate an expectation that resonates with the reader.

Studies have shown that if you highlight a gap in someone's knowledge, especially in a subject that are interested in, you can pique their curiosity. Their interest becomes peaked.

Imagine you are a skilled musician, but aren't making much money. Notice how the following headline grabs your attention:

Why Lousy Musicians Are Getting Good Gigs: How You Can Get Those Gigs instead!

This headline garners interest because it violates the expectation that lousy musicians can be successful. It also implies that lousy musicians are onto something which you may not be, and so thusly you are missing out on something. This headline draws your interest because it promises to let you in on the thing that you don't know about, but others do.

9. Use Keywords!

Another insider trick is to use "keywords" at the bottom of your ad. Keywords are additional search words that are not part of your description that buyers might also use to search for your item. These keywords don't have to specifically relevant to your item, but if you want to lead someone to your ad because you think someone searching for something similar might also be interested, then using a keyword could help improve your search results.

Your keyword does not even have to apply 100% specifically to your item. As an example, say I was looking to sell a guitar. It is not a Fender guitar, but it has a fender style body and many features that you might also find on a Fender guitar. However if someone is searching only for a Fender, then they will miss my ad completely unless I specifically mention the brand Fender in my listing. And, even though the searcher was actually looking for a Fender guitar, they might see that the guitar I have is one they might like to have instead or in addition to one they were looking for.

Other keywords to include besides other brands are misspellings. Think about it, how many possible mis-spellings might be out there. Is it Ping Pong, ping-pong, or pingpong? What about Pin Ball, pin-ball or Pinball? Or is it misspellings, miss spellings, mis-spellings, or mis spellings. There are people who make a living by buying mis-spelled websites. Is it Craigslist, Craigs'list, craigs'list or Craig's List? You get the idea....

So let's use the following example. Say I have a Lotus guitar for sale. Lotus guitar were usually copies of better-known, up-market brand-name guitars, such as the Gibson Les Paul and the Fender Stratocaster. The quality of the instruments was very good for the price (usually around US$400–$900).

Here's how the "Keyword" line at the bottom of the listing might read:

Keywords: Fender,Stratocaster, Lotis, stratocster,fener

If anyone searches for any of those words-even the misspelled ones-the search engine will still find my listing and present it when someone types any of things in for a search.

People who are deeply invested in Search engine Optimization (also known as SEO) will spend a fair amount of time researching misspelled words to include in their keywords so that search engines will turn up results even if someone misspells or mis-keys an entry. Usually people who get into that much detail are doing SEO for websites, as that is where it very critical for businesses to get high search engine rankings. However, this knowledge can always be applied to any search engine for any site.

If you're interested in exploring this further do an internet search on "keyword typo generator." You will find numerous websites specifically dedicated to helping to identify those mis-spelled keywords. Here's an example of what one of those sites look for, using the parameter of "skip letter" for the brand name Fender. Note the many options for producing common mis-spellings. You can also do combinations if you want to check every possible angle:

Keyword Typos Generator

Use this tool to generate a list of typos and common misspellings for pay per click ads and domain names. This software/script should help you in the generation of a low competition keywords to save money on PPC ads.

Enter one word or phrase per line

fender

☑ Skip letter
☐ Double letters
☐ Reverse letters
☐ Skip spaces
☐ Missed key
☐ Inserted key

[generate typos]

```
ender
fnder
feder
fener
fendr
fende
```

(source: http://tools.ppcblog.com/spelling/keywords-typos.cgi)

Chapter Four: Selling FAQs

When should I post my listings?

The theory here is that you want to be near the top of the page when the most eyeballs are on Craigslist looking at ads. Typically that is weekends and evenings. There is no strict rule that you have to adhere to, but if you think of it that is common sense. Use your best judgement. Sometimes I will put up listings any time of the day just to get them going. There is also some evidence that there are early morning browsers as well, so that may be another time to consider beginning your listings.

Typically, weekend posts tend to do better than weekday posts, and I always like to post mine around late-afternoon, when people are home from errands, but before they head out to dinner. When it comes to results it's also important to remember where you live. For example, I live in a very rural region of NH, and so the number of responses I get are very few compared to someone who lives in a more populous area. I know this because I have been in other areas of the country and run Craigslist postings and was overwhelmed by the speed and number of responses-I was not used to that at all. Things that might have taken me several weeks to sell in NH sold in a matter of only hours in a large suburb of Chicago.

One negotiation caveat. If your item is popular and you have received a number of email inquiries, you may get counteroffers from one or more of them on your price. If you are firm with your price, (or want to get as close as you can to your asking price), explain to any low offers that you will accept only full price because there has been a lot interest shown in the item. You might be surprised by how an offer suddenly increases if a buyer realizes they may be in competition with other buyers.

What time is best for posting listings?

Post in the late afternoon

Most people get on the internet after they get home from work. There is a definite spike in internet use after 5 p.m. The best time to post your ad is after 5 p.m. If you post earlier, your ad could already move far enough down the page that it will not be easily seen. It's all a guessing game of course, but it does stand to reason that you will get more traffic later in the day.

What if I need to sell an item fast?

Set a deadline.

One time I needed to sell something quick, so I stated "Needs picked up by Tuesday" in my ad. I had serious buyers responding to me right away. It put enough pressure on them to act now and to not mess around with negotiating. I've done it ever since anytime I wanted to move something quickly.

I would also add the following tips:

Be real about your time frame. If you say you want to get rid of something by next Tuesday, then mean it. If it doesn't sell then give it away or put it in a yard sale. BUT DON'T RE-LIST IT. At least not for a while. Otherwise, there is not really an urgent need to sell, is there?

If you set your deadline for 1-2 days out, then expect to negotiate as the deadline looms near.
If you set the deadline to be 3-6 days away it gives you a bit more leverage to negotiate with.

What about the question of location:....Should I post in more than one region?

If you happen to live, as I do in close proximity to several different CL geographies, you may be thinking about putting your ad on multiple community sites. For example, I live in NH, but within about 20 miles of the VT border, so I wondered if I should post my listings on both the NH & VT CL sites?

One problem though, this is against Craigslist rules. According to CL:

"Can I post my ad on more than one Craigslist site?

Please choose just ONE local Craigslist site for which your ad is most relevant—generally the site closest to you. If your ad is equally relevant to all locations, your ad does not belong on Craigslist. Please find another service. Posting the same ad to multiple locations on Craigslist is prohibited."

There are ways of getting around this, using listing services or virtual assistants. But the effort to do this requires more dedication than it is worth for the average CL like me. So I stick to the rules. I would prefer my ads not to be blocked or removed ("Ghosting is what veteran CL users call that.)

If your ad gets blocked or removed, you have to redo all the content of your account since you will have to make a new one. I don't think the risk is worth the effort because I am not a big fan of re-doing work I've already done.

One alternative that does work is if you create a totally different ad for your item (make sure the title especially is different) you should be OK to post in another region. But you will have to create a new and unique ad for each region that you post in. If you post identical ads it will be considered spam and will be removed. Theoretically you could also get tagged if someone realizes that it is the same item and flags you on it. That is unlikely-but if you have competitors they may stoop to that level. The choice is yours on how you think it is best to handle this.

Tracking Results – In 2013 Craigslist made changes to their policies which basically disallowed the use of HTML code that tracking services use to create page counters. The reason that they did this was that many marketers were doing A/B tests to see which of their ads would perform better based on headline, title, time of posting etc. Because CL is free, they were not limited to the amount of variances they could put on CL-so there potentially unlimited number of ads that could be put up for the same item or service. This got out of hand as it became basically spam, and a nuisance that filled CL with all kind of unnecessary listings. So there is no reliable way that I know of to see how many times someone has visited one of your listings. (There are some super sophisticated ways of doing it, but in my view, it's more trouble than it's worth.)

My conclusion is that it is not an easy prospect to keep track of which versions of your ads are getting more clicks. As I mentioned, there are workarounds that I have seen but they require extra effort that in my opinion are beyond the knowledge level (or desire) of the average CL

Chapter Five: How to Safely Negotiate the Seller Contact Sequence

Here's what to expect in the communication sequence of making a sale on CL.

1. You Put up your ad
2. Someone Contacts you, likely asks if item is available and will you take x$ for it.
3. Beware the scam inquiry! (See the section on scams for more details)
4. You reply yes, but you have several other inquiries for the item. You would like to sell it for as close to your original listing price as you can. However, if you were willing to offer (your counter-offer price) I would agree to sell it to you right now.
5. If you get no response back, that's OK, they're not a serious buyer. Move on.
6. If they counter-offer your counteroffer you can agree or not agree. The faster their response is, the more serious their interest is. You can decide. How fast do you want to move the item? You have to trust your instincts here. If you feel like you should hold out for more money then do so, even if you have to walk away from the deal. If you are motivated to sell then by all means- agree to terms!
7. Make contact to complete the sale-but make sure you follow suggested security terms:

According to Craigslist:

"Please take the same common sense precautions online as you would offline.

When meeting someone for the first time, please remember to:

Insist on a public meeting place like a cafe, bank, or shopping center. Do not meet in a secluded place, or invite strangers into your home. Be especially careful buying/selling high value items.
Tell a friend or family member where you're going. Take your cell phone along if you have one.
Consider having a friend accompany you. Trust your instincts.
Taking these simple precautions helps make Craigslist safer for everyone.

Sometimes, if you have a large item you have no choice but to have the buyer come to your house. In that instance what I usually do is to enlist my good friend Google to help me research the individual. Most of the time you should be able to get enough information from the potential buyer to be able to do some research on them before you interact. If anything seems suspicious, by all means err on the side of caution.

Avoiding Scams:

Deal locally, face-to-face —follow this one rule and avoid 99% of scam attempts.

Do not extend payment to anyone you have not met in person.
Beware offers involving shipping - deal with locals you can meet in person.
Never wire funds (e.g. Western Union) - anyone who asks you to is a scammer.
Don't accept cashier/certified checks or money orders - banks cash fakes, then hold you responsible.
Transactions are between users only, no third party provides a "guarantee".
Never give out financial info (bank account, social security, PayPal account, etc.).
Do not rent or purchase sight-unseen—that amazing "deal" may not exist.
Refuse background/credit checks until you have met landlord/employer in person."

(Source: Craigslist website)

A Few More Words About Safety:

There are some folks who are fearful of buying or selling on Craigslist mostly due to a few isolated cases that were widely publicized by the media. However if you take a few simple common-sense precautions you should not run into any problems. It is usually a good idea to have at least one phone conversation with a buyer. That way you get at least some sense that they're real.

This is where I try to determine my level of comfort/safety before I consider meeting up the individual in person. If I am selling a high priced item, or if I don't feel completely comfortable after discussion, I won't invite them to make a transaction at my house. I don't want someone deciding that I am a beehive of valuable items.

Instead encourage a buyer to meet at a public location like the police station parking lot, a coffee shop or a bank. In fact many police departments even encourage using designated areas near or on their property to conduct safe transactions. If I follow that approach I don't have to let anyone know where I live, and the buyer also feels they're in a safe environment to make a cash transaction.

If you are selling large items, like furniture or refrigerators, you will have no alternative but to have people come see the item where it is. So give that some thought before proceeding to list large items.
If you are selling items from your home it's a good idea to have a staging area like a garage or entryway. That way they can see the item without seeing the rest of your house, or tracking mud or whatever throughout your house.

Also, remember that it is good to put your buyer at ease. Dress neat, be friendly and courteous. You don't want to creep your buyer out! FIRST IMPRESSIONS ARE EVERYTHING. Don't signal to your buyer that you are there for anything other than a professional business transaction. This will help with the negotiation stage and maybe if there is some rapport, you might have other items they are interested as well. (Either now or in the future.)

As far as scams, it is also a good idea to review the following information from Craigslist:

"Recognizing scams

Most scams attempts involve one or more of the following:

Email or text from someone that is not local to your area. Vague initial inquiry, e.g. asking about "the item." Poor grammar/spelling. Western Union, Money Gram, cashier check, money order, PayPal, shipping, escrow service, or a "guarantee." Inability or refusal to meet face-to-face to complete the transaction.

Examples of Scams

1. Someone claims your transaction is guaranteed, that a buyer/seller is officially certified, OR that a third party of any kind will handle or provide protection for a payment:

These claims are fraudulent, as transactions are between users only. The scammer will often send an official looking (but fake) email that appears to come from Craigslist or another third party, offering a guarantee, certifying a seller, or pretending to handle payments.

2. Distant person offers a genuine-looking (but fake) cashier's check:

You receive an email or text (examples below) offering to buy your item, pay for your services in advance, or rent your apartment, sight unseen and without meeting you in person. A cashier's check is offered for your sale item as a deposit for an apartment or for your services. Value of cashier's check often far exceeds your item—scammer offers to "trust" you, and asks you to wire the balance via money transfer service.

Banks will cash fake checks AND THEN HOLD YOU RESPONSIBLE WHEN THE CHECK FAILS TO CLEAR, sometimes including criminal prosecution. Scams often pretend to involve a 3rd party (shipping agent, business associate, etc.).

3. Someone requests wire service payment via Western Union or MoneyGram:

Deal often seems too good to be true, price is too low, or rent is below market, etc.
Scam "bait" items include apartments, laptops, TVs, cell phones, tickets, other high value items.
Scammer may (falsely) claim a confirmation code from you is needed before he can withdraw your money.

Common countries currently include: Nigeria, Romania, UK, and Netherlands—but could be anywhere.
Rental may be local, but owner is "travelling" or "relocating" and needs you to wire money abroad.
Scammer may pretend to be unable to speak by phone (scammers prefer to operate by text/email).

4. Distant person offers to send you a cashier's check or money order and then have you wire money:

This is ALWAYS a scam in our experience—the cashier's check is FAKE. Sometimes accompanies an offer of merchandise, sometimes not. Scammer often asks for your name, address, etc. for printing on the fake check. Deal often seems too good to be true.

5. Distant seller suggests use of an online escrow service:

Most online escrow sites are FRAUDULENT and operated by scammers. For more info, do a google search on "fake escrow" or "escrow fraud."

6. Distant seller asks for a partial payment upfront, after which they will ship goods:

He says he trusts you with the partial payment. He may say he has already shipped the goods.
Deal often sounds too good to be true.

7. Foreign company offers you a job receiving payments from customers, then wiring funds:

Foreign company may claim it is unable to receive payments from its customers directly. You are typically offered a percentage of payments received. This kind of "position" may be posted as a job, or offered to you via email. "

(source:www.craigslist.com)

Chapter Six: The Finish Line

Final sale:

Of course be courteous and help load/unload items. As far as payment, I personally don't like large denomination cash bills- If someone is paying in large bills, don't be afraid to double-check whether they're real bills and have them verified at a nearby bank. Again, if you state your payment policy up front when you are discussing the sale with the buyer, there should be no surprises when the actual transaction takes place.

What to do if you're not getting responses for your item:

It may be that you are putting prices on your item that are a bit too high. I do this on purpose-it is a part of my strategy, but that is only if I'm not in a hurry to sell an item. I always start with a high price if I am unsure of what the market value is after doing my homework in comparison pricing on eBay and CL for similar items. If I find a similar item to mine after doing that comparison, I may start at the highest sold price and work my way down from there.

I keep a spreadsheet that lists each item, the date I listed and what my opening asking price was. Over the course of time, I slowly bring down the price if it doesn't sell. Again each time I make a change I note the date I changed the price and what the price was reduced to. That way I can make a rough estimate of about when I think it's time to reduce the price if need be.

Another secret as alluded to previously-if you decide you want to move your item, rather than waiting out the market to fit a good price, add "or Best Offer" to your price. Then at least you should get some offers. But expect some of them to not be that serious. However, don't write them off right away. Some of the lowballs can be legit. If they have enough interest to even contact you, that interest has potential to be cultivated, even if the offer didn't seem sincere at first. It's your job to figure that out....

Conclusion:

Craigslist is a great nationwide garage sale, and there is much to be found for deals for both buyers and sellers. If you exercise proper precautions you will find that everyone you meet is generally interested and enthusiastic about making mutually beneficial transactions. It's a great way to move some of the extra items you have, make a few extra dollars, or even a potential living by selling goods on Craigslist.

We like it because it takes away a lot of the third party element that costs you money in making a sale. There's no final value fees, listing fees, or shipping headaches. The customers are real, and often times can be a source of repeat business or other referrals. So, take these tips in mind and we wish you the best of luck in making Craigslist a great source for your own benefit!